# Abbreviations

| | | | |
|---|---|---|---|
| **approx** | approximately | **patt** | pattern |
| **beg** | begin/beginning | **pc** | popcorn |
| **bet** | between | **pm** | place marker |
| **BL** | back loop(s) | **prev** | previous |
| **BP** | back post | **rem** | remain/remaining |
| **BPdc** | back post double crochet | **rep** | repeat(s) |
| **CC** | contrasting color | **rev sc** | reverse single crochet |
| **ch** | chain | **rnd(s)** | round(s) |
| **ch-** | refers to chain or space previously made, e.g., ch-1 space | **RS** | right side(s) |
| | | **sc** | single crochet |
| **ch lp** | chain loop | **sc2tog** | single crochet 2 stitches together |
| **ch-sp** | chain space | | |
| **CL** | cluster | **sk** | skip |
| **cm** | centimeter(s) | **Sl st** | slip stitch |
| **cont** | continue | **sp(s)** | space(s) |
| **dc** | double crochet | **st(s)** | stitch(es) |
| **dc2tog** | double crochet 2 stitches together | **tbl** | through back loop |
| | | **tch** | turning chain |
| **dec** | decrease/decreases/decreasing | **tfl** | through front loop |
| | | **tog** | together |
| **FL** | front loop(s) | **tr** | triple crochet |
| **foll** | follow/follows/following | **WS** | wrong side(s) |
| **FP** | front post | **yd** | yard(s) |
| **FPdc** | front post double crochet | **yo** | yarn over |
| **g** | gram(s) | **yoh** | yarn over hook |
| **hdc** | half double crochet | **[ ]** | Work instructions within brackets as many times as directed |
| **inc** | increase/increases/increasing | | |
| | | **( )** | At end of row, indicates total number of stitches worked |
| **lp(s)** | loop(s) | | |
| **m** | meter(s) | ***** | Repeat instructions following the single asterisk as directed |
| **MC** | main color | | |
| **mm** | millimeter(s) | ****** | Repeat instructions between asterisks as many times as directed or repeat from a given set of instructions |
| **oz** | ounce(s) | | |
| **p** | picot | | |

# Dainty Shells Scarf

Feminine in a plush chenille yarn, this scarf showcases the pretty shell stitch. Front post and back post double crochet adds a subtle depth and definition to the overall pattern, and the shell stitch appears again in the edging.

**YARN**
Medium-weight cotton/rayon chenille yarn
5.25 oz (150 g)/360 yd (330 m)

**HOOK**
Size 8/H (5 mm)

**STITCHES USED**
Double crochet
Front post double crochet
Back post double crochet

**GAUGE**
3½ shell clusters = 4" (10 cm) on 8/H hook

**NOTION**
Tapestry needle

**FINISHED SIZE**
5" (13 cm) wide and 60" (152 cm) long

Front post and back post double crochet stitches form ridges between shells.

## SCARF

First half of scarf is worked first, then second half is picked up from beg of first half and worked out to the end.

**Foundation row:** Ch 26. Starting in fifth ch from hook, work [2 dc, ch 1, 2 dc] in same ch (shell cluster), * sk 2 ch, work 1 dc in next ch, sk 2 ch, work [2 dc, ch 1, 2 dc] in next ch. Rep from * across, 1 dc in last ch, ch 3, turn.

**Row 1:** * Work [2 dc, ch 1, 2 dc] in ch-1 sp, FPdc in dc, rep from * across, [2 dc, ch 1, 2 dc] in ch-1 sp, dc in top of tch, ch 3, turn.

**Row 2:** * Work [2 dc, ch 1, 2 dc] in ch-1 sp, BPdc in dc, rep from * across, [2 dc, ch 1, 2 dc] in ch-1 sp, dc in top of tch, ch 3, turn.

Rep rows 1 and 2 for 28" (71 cm) from beg, end row 2. Work edging as foll:

## EDGING

**Row 1:** * Work [3 dc, ch 2, 3 dc] in ch-1 sp, FPdc in dc, rep from * across, [3 dc, ch 2, 3 dc] in ch-1 sp, dc in top of tch, ch 3, turn.

Both ends of the scarf are finished with scalloped edging.

**Row 2:** * Work [4 dc, ch 2, 4 dc] in ch-2 sp, BPdc in dc, rep from * across, [4 dc, ch 2, 4 dc] in ch-2 sp, dc in top of tch, ch 3, turn.

**Row 3:** * Work [4 dc, ch 2, 4 dc] in ch-2 sp, FPdc in dc, rep from * across, [4 dc, ch 2, 4 dc] in ch-2 sp, dc in top of tch, ch 3, turn. Fasten off.

## SECOND HALF OF SCARF
Join yarn in right corner of beg of scarf, ch 3.

**Foundation row:** Work [2 dc, ch 1, 2 dc] in same ch as cluster, * sk 2 ch, work 1 dc in same ch as dc, sk 2 ch, work [2 dc, ch 1, 2 dc] in same ch as cluster. Rep from * across, 1 dc in same ch as last dc, ch 3, turn.

Cont with row 1 of scarf, rep scarf and edging as for first half. Fasten off.

## FINISHING
Weave in ends using tapestry needle.

# Raspberry Puff Scarf

A soft, lacy, puff-stitch pattern in a beautifully draping ribbon yarn

creates a scarf for any season. Make it bright and bold, or in a soft

shade for a vintage look. A trellis shell stitch pattern finishes the ends.

**YARN**
Medium-weight rayon ribbon
5.25 oz (150 g)/225 yd (207 m)

**HOOK**
Size 8/H (5 mm)

**STITCHES USED**
Single crochet
Double crochet
Puff stitch

**GAUGE**
3 puff sts = 4" (10 cm) on 8/H hook

**NOTION**
Tapestry needle

**FINISHED SIZE**
5" (13 cm) wide and 46" (117 cm) long

Rayon ribbon yarn is hooked in double-crochet clusters called puff stitches.

## SCARF

Scarf is worked lengthwise.

**Foundation row:** Ch 129. Starting in fourth ch from hook, work 1 dc, * ch 2, sk next ch, 1 sc in next ch, ch 2, sk next ch, 1 dc in each of next 3 ch, rep from * across, 1 dc in each of last 2 ch, ch 3 (counts as dc now and throughout), turn.

**Row 1:** Sk first st, 1 dc in next st, * ch 3, 1 dc in first dc of 3-dc cluster, 1 puff st in next dc, 1 dc in next dc, rep from * across, ch 3, 1 dc in next dc, 1 dc in top of tch, ch 3, turn.

**Row 2:** Sk first st, 1 dc in next st, * ch 2, 1 sc in ch-3 sp, ch 2, 1 dc in next dc, 1 dc in puff st, 1 dc in next dc, rep from * across, ch 2, 1 sc in ch-3 sp, ch 2, 1 dc in next dc, 1 dc in top of tch, ch 3, turn.

Rep rows 1 and 2 four times more (5 puff st rows in all), end row 2, do not fasten off. Ch 1, turn to work along end of scarf, work edging as foll:

Main scarf is worked side to side. Several rows of lacy openwork are added at each end.

## EDGING

**Foundation row:** Work 25 sc across end of scarf, ch 3, turn.

**Row 1:** Work 2 dc in first st, sk 2 sts, 1 sc in next st, ch 6, sk 5 sts, 1 sc in next st, sk 2 sts, 5 dc in next sc (shell made), sk 2 sts, 1 sc in next sc, ch 6, sk 5 sts, 1 sc in next st, ch 2, sk 2 sts, 3 dc in last st, ch 1, turn.

**Row 2:** Work 1 sc in first st, ch 5, 1 sc in ch-5 sp, ch 5, 1 sc in third dc of shell, ch 5, 1 sc in ch-5 sp, ch 5, 1 sc in top of tch, ch 5, turn.

**Row 3:** Work *1 sc in ch-5 sp, 5 dc in next st, 1 sc in ch-5 sp, ch 5, 1 sc in ch-5 sp, 5 dc in next st, 1 sc in ch-5 sp, ch 2, 1 dc in top of tch, ch 1, turn.

**Row 4:** Work 1 sc in first st, ch 5, 1 sc in third dc of shell, ch 5, 1 sc in ch-5 sp, ch 5, 1 sc in third dc of shell, ch 5, 1 sc in third ch of tch, ch 3, turn.

**Row 5:** Work 2 dc in first st, 1 sc in ch-5 sp, ch 5, 1 sc in ch-5 sp, 5 dc in next st, 1 sc in ch-5 sp, ch 5, 1 sc in ch-5 sp, 3 dc in top of tch, ch 1, turn.

Rep rows 2–5 once more, then rep rows 2–3, fasten off.

Work other end of scarf to correspond.

## FINISHING

Weave in ends using tapestry needle.

# Pico Mesh Scarf

Pamper yourself with a silk-blend scarf in an elegant and easy picot mesh stitch. The scarf is soft, luxurious, and sophisticated. For a crisper, more casual look, try this scarf in a shiny cotton/rayon blend.

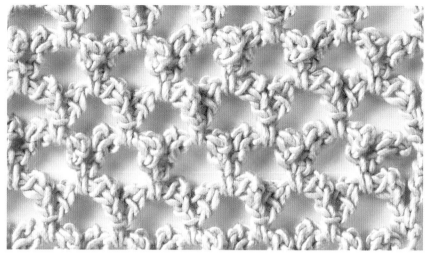

Luxurious silk/wool blend yarn hooked in a dainty picot mesh pattern.

## SCARF

**Foundation row:** Ch 32. Work 1 sc in second ch from hook* [ch 4, 1 sc in third ch from hook (picot made)] twice, ch 1, sk 4 chs, 1 sc in next ch, rep from * across (6 ch-4 sps), ch 9 (counts as 1 dc, ch 4), turn.

**Row 1:** Work 1 sc in third ch from hook, ch 1, 1 sc in center of 2 picots, * [ch 4, 1 sc in 3rd ch from hook] twice, ch 1, 1 sc between 2 picots, rep from * across, ch 4, 1 sc in 3rd ch from hook, 1 dtr in last sc, ch 1, turn.

**Row 2:** Work 1 sc in first dtr, * [ch 4, 1 sc in third ch from hook] twice, ch 1, 1 sc between 2 picots, rep from * across, 1 sc in fifth ch of beg ch 9.

Rep rows 1 and 2 for 50" (127 cm) end row 2, fasten off.

Join yarn in the right-hand corner of other end of scarf, ch 9, work rows 1 and 2 once only, as foll:

**Row 1:** Work 1 sc in third ch from hook, ch 1, 1 sc in next sp, * [ch 4, 1 sc in third ch from hook] twice, ch 1, 1 sc in next sp, rep from * across, ch 4, 1 sc in third ch from hook, ch 1, 1 dtr in last st, ch 1, turn.

**Row 2:** Work 1 sc in first dtr, * [ch 4, 1 sc in third ch from hook] twice, ch 1, 1 sc between 2 picots, rep from * across, 1 sc in the fifth ch of beg ch 9. Fasten off.

## FINISHING

Weave in ends using tapestry needle.

---

### YARN
Medium-weight silk/wool blend yarn
3.5 oz (100 g)/220 yd (202 m)

### HOOK
Size 8/H (5 mm)

### STITCHES USED
Single crochet
Double triple crochet

### GAUGE
3½ clusters = 4" (10 cm) on 8/H hook

### NOTION
Tapestry needle

### FINISHED SIZE
5" (13 cm) wide and 50" (127 cm) long

# Garden Trellis Scarf

The unusual stitch in this scarf looks like a trellis of flowers. The effect

is achieved by combining clusters of triple crochet with openwork.

**YARN**
Medium-weight cotton/rayon
blend bouclé yarn
8 oz (225 g)/585 yd (538 m)

**HOOK**
Size 8/H (5 mm)

**STITCHES USED**
Single crochet
Double crochet
Triple crochet
Triple crochet 2 together
Double triple crochet

**GAUGE**
2 clusters = 4" (10 cm)
on 8/H hook

**NOTION**
Tapestry needle

**FINISHED SIZE**
6" (15 cm) wide and 64"
(162 cm) long

Cotton/rayon bouclé yarn crocheted in alternating rows of flowers and lattice.

## SCARF

**Foundation row:** Ch 35. Starting in eighth ch from hook, work 1 dc, * ch 2, sk 2 ch, 1 dc into next ch, rep from * (10 ch-2 sps), ch 1, turn.

**Row 1:** Work 1 sc in first dc, * ch 9, sk 1 dc, [1 sc, ch 4, 1 tr2tog] in next dc, sk 1 dc, [1 tr2tog, ch 4, 1 sc] in next dc, rep from * once, ch 9, sk 1 dc, 1 sc in third ch of tch (3 ch-9 loops, 2 clusters), ch 10 (counts as dtr, ch 4), turn.

**Row 2:** Work 1 sc in first ch-9 sp, * ch 4, [1 tr2tog, ch 4, 1 Sl st, ch 4, 1 tr2tog] in top of next tr2tog, ch 4, 1 sc in next ch-9 sp, rep from * once, ch 4, 1 dtr in last sc, (6 ch-4 lps, 2 clusters), ch 1, turn.

**Row 3:** Work 1 sc in first dtr, * ch 5, 1 sc in top of next tr2tog, rep from * across, ch 5, 1 sc in sixth ch of tch, (5 ch-5 sp), ch 5, (counts as 1 dc, ch 2), turn.

**Row 4:** Work 1 dc in next ch-5 sp, ch 2, 1 dc in next sc, *ch 2, 1 dc in next ch-5 sp, ch 2, 1 dc in next sc, rep from * across (10 ch-2 sps), ch 1, turn.

Rep rows 1–4 for 62" from beg, end row 4. Work edging as foll:

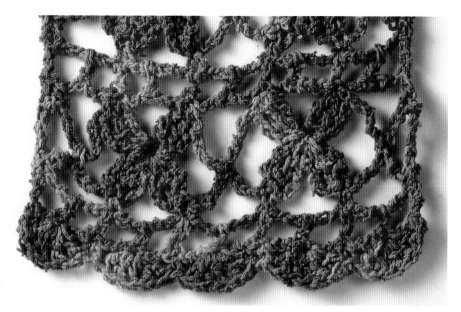

Shell edging finishes the scarf ends.

## EDGING

**Row 1:** Sk first dc, work 5 dc in next dc, 1 sc in next dc, * 5 dc in next dc, 1 sc in next dc, rep from * across (5 shells), fasten off.

Join yarn in right-hand corner at other end of scarf, ch 1, rep row 1 of edging.

## FINISHING

Weave in ends using tapestry needle.

# Peaches and Cream Scarf

This summery peaches-and-cream scarf gets its airy texture from a lofty

yarn and a shell-stitch pattern.

**YARN**

Lightweight cotton/rayon blend yarn

4 oz (113 g)/220 yd (202 m)

**HOOK**

Size 6/G (4.5 mm)

**STITCHES USED**

Single crochet

Double crochet

Triple crochet

Triple crochet 3 together

**GAUGE**

1 tr3tog cluster = 2" (10 cm) on 6/G hook

**NOTION**

Tapestry needle

**FINISHED SIZE**

5" (13 cm) wide and 48" (122 cm) long

Leaf-shaped clusters are worked in both directions from a center foundation row.

## SCARF

First half of scarf is worked first, then second half is picked up from beg of first half and worked out to the end.

**Foundation row:** Ch 22. Starting in fifth ch from hook, work [3 dc, ch 2, 3 dc] in ch, ch 4, sk 7 ch, [1 dc, ch 4, 1 dc] in next ch, ch 4, sk 7 ch, [3 dc, ch 2, 3 dc] in next ch, 1 dc in last ch,  ch 3 (counts as dc now and throughout), turn.

**Row 1:** Work [3 dc, ch 3, 3 dc] in next ch-2 sp, ch 2, sk 1 ch-4 sp, [1 tr3 tog, ch 3] 3 times in next ch-4 sp, 1 tr3tog in same sp, ch 2, sk 1 ch-4 sp, [3 dc, ch 2, 3 dc] in next ch-2 sp, 1 dc in top of tch, ch 3, turn.

**Row 2:** Work [3 dc, ch 2, 3 dc] in next ch-2 sp, ch 3, sk 1 ch-2 sp, [2 sc in next ch-3 sp, ch 3] twice, 2 sc in next ch-3 sp, ch 3, sk 1 ch-2 sp [3 dc, ch 2, 3 dc] in last ch-2 sp, 1 dc in top of tch, ch 3, turn.

**Row 3:** Work [3 dc, ch 2, 3 dc] in next ch-2 sp, ch 4, sk 1 ch-3 sp, 2 sc in next ch-3 sp, ch 3, 2 sc in next ch-3 sp, ch 4, sk 1 ch-3 sp, [3 dc, ch 2, 3 dc] in last ch-2 sp, 1 dc in top of tch, ch 3, turn.

**Row 4:** Work [3 dc, ch 2, 3 dc] in next ch-2 sp, ch 4, sk 1 ch-3 sp, [1 dc, ch 4, 1 dc] in next ch-3 sp, ch 4, sk 1 ch-3 sp, [3 dc, ch 2, 3 dc] in next ch-2 sp, 1 dc in top of tch, ch 3, turn.

Rep rows 1–4 for 24" (61 cm) from beg, fasten off.

Strands of cotton and rayon twisted together give the yarn a two-tone tweed look.

## SECOND HALF OF SCARF

Join yarn in right corner of beg of scarf, ch 3.

**Foundation row:** Work [3 dc, ch 2, 3 dc] in same ch as dc cluster, ch 4, sk 7 ch, [1 dc, ch 4, 1 dc] in same ch as dcs, ch 4, sk 7 ch, [3 dc, ch 2, 3 dc] in same ch as dc cluster, sk 1 ch, 1 dc in same ch as dc.

Rep rows 1–4 for 24" (61 cm) from beg, fasten off.

## FINISHING

Weave in ends using tapestry needle.

# Blooming Ascot

Step into spring with this soft, feminine ascot. A slit at one end of the scarf allows you to pull the other end through for an adjustable fit, and a flower adds a decorative touch.

**YARN**

Medium-weight cotton/nylon blend yarn

3.5 oz (100 g)/194 yd (180 m)

**HOOK**

Size 8/H (5 mm)

**STITCHES USED**

Single crochet

Double crochet

**GAUGE**

12½ dc = 4" (10 cm) on 8/H hook

**NOTION**

Tapestry needle

**FINISHED SIZE**

7" (18 cm) wide and 44" (112 cm) long

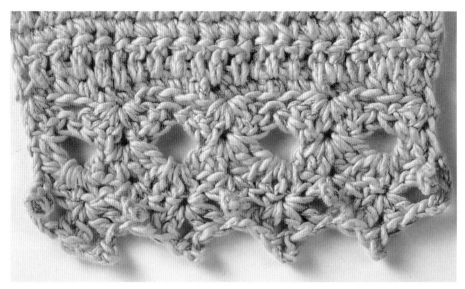

Scarf is alternating rows of single and double crochet with feminine picot edging at the ends.

## SCARF

**Foundation row:** Ch 22. Starting in second ch from hook, work 1 sc in each ch across (21 sc), ch 3 (counts as dc now and throughout), turn.

**Row 1:** Sk first st, work 1 dc in each of next 19 sts, 1 dc in tch (21 dc), ch 1 (counts as sc now and throughout), turn.

**Row 2:** Sk first st, work 1 sc in each of next 19 sts, 1 sc in top of tch (21 sc), ch 3, turn.

Rep rows 1 and 2 for 33" (84 cm) from beg.

Form opening as foll:

**Next row:** Beg with row 1, work 1 dc in each of next 9 sts, ch 1, turn. Cont to rep rows 1 and 2 over these 10 sts for 2" (5 cm), end row 2, fasten off.

Sk 1 st at center of scarf at opening edge, rejoin yarn, ch 3. Beg with row 1, work 1 dc in each of 9 rem sts. Cont to rep rows 1 and 2 over these 10 sts for 2" (5 cm), end at outside edge and with row 2. Ch 3, turn, work 10 dc (first opening half), ch 1, 10 dc across rem sts (second opening half).

Rep rows 1 and 2 across all 21 sts for 40" (102 cm) from beg, end row 2. Ch 3, turn, work edging as foll:

## EDGING

**Row 1:** Work 2 dc in same st as tch, * sk 4 st, [3 dc, ch 2, 3 dc] in next st (shell made); rep from * across, sk 4 sc, 3 dc in top of tch, ch 2, turn.

**Row 2:** Work 2 dc in same st as tch, * ch 1, [3 dc, ch 2, 3 dc] in ch-2 sp of next shell; rep from * across, ch 1, 3 dc in top of tch, ch 4, turn.

Crocheted flower is sewn onto the scarf next to the opening.

**Row 3:** Work 1 Sl st in fourth ch from hook, 1 sc in same st as tch, * 3 dc in ch-1 sp, [1 sc, ch 4, Sl st in fourth ch from hook, 1 sc] in ch-2 sp of next shell (picot group made). Rep from * once, 3 dc in ch-1 sp, 1 sc in top of tch, ch 4, Sl st in fourth ch from hook, Sl st in last sc worked, ch 5, turn.

**Row 4:** * Work [2 dc, ch 4, Sl st in fourth ch from hook, 2 dc] in center dc of 3-dc group, rep from * across, ch 5, sl st in last st, fasten off.

Work other end of scarf to correspond.

### FLOWER
**Foundation rnd:** Ch 1 (center), ch 3 (counts as dc), work 11 dc in beg ch, join with Sl st to top of beg ch 3 (12 dc).

**Rnd 1:** Ch 1, work [1 sc, ch 1, 1 sc] in same st as ch 1, * ch 1, [1 sc, ch 1, 1 sc] in FL of next st; rep from * around, ch 1, join with Sl st in both loops of first sc (center petals made).

**Rnd 2:** Holding center petals forward and working in BL of foundation rnd, [1 sc, ch 2, 1 dc, 1 tr, ch 3, Sl st in first ch of ch-3, 1 tr, 1 dc, ch 2] in each st around, fasten off.

### FINISHING
**1.** With the opening end of the scarf pointing toward you, position flower on the left side of the opening, centering it on the opening. Using tapestry needle and the loose end from beg of flower, sew flower securely onto scarf.
**2.** Weave in ends using tapestry needle.